Wouuff!
wouuff!

Thank you to our amazing family and many friends who have helped and supported this book from the beginning.

The Twins Mia & Mateo - Daddy's Little Helpers
Les Jumeaux Mia & Mateo - Papa et ses Petits Assistants
By Anne-Marie Martens and Marjorie Joys
Illustrated by Vanessa Alexandre

For inquiries, sales, or permission requests contact the author:
Anne-Marie Martens at annemariebookwriter@gmail.com

First published in 2017
Manufactured in China

The illustrations in the book were created using acrylics, watercolor and digital art.

The Twins - Les Jumeaux

Mia & Mateo

Daddy's Little Helpers
Papa et ses Petits Assistants

By Anne-Marie Martens & Marjorie Joys - Illustrated by Vanessa Alexandre

Today, Daddy wants to wash his car. He has prepared buckets, sponges, brushes and the vacuum cleaner. Twins, Mia and Mateo, are playing in front of the house with their dog, Patchy.

Aujourd'hui, Papa veut laver sa voiture. Il a préparé des seaux, des éponges, des brosses et l'aspirateur. Les jumeaux, Mia et Mateo, jouent devant la maison avec leur chien Patchy.

"Can we help you Daddy?" asked Mateo. "With the three of us, it will go faster."

– On peut t'aider Papa? demande Mateo. A trois, on ira plus vite.

Daddy hesitates, because he is not sure they are up for the big challenge.
"Come on Daddy. We are big enough to help you. We can do it," said Mateo.

Papa hésite un peu car il n'est pas convaincu.
– Allez Papa. On est assez grands maintenant pour t'aider. On peut le faire, dit Mateo.

“Okay,” Daddy said, “here are your buckets and your sponges. I am counting on you to help me make the car clean and shine. You wash the outside and I’ll vacuum the inside.”

– D’accord, dit Papa, voici vos seaux et vos éponges. Je compte sur vous pour m’aider; la voiture doit être propre et brillante. Vous lavez l’extérieur et je vais aspirer l’intérieur.

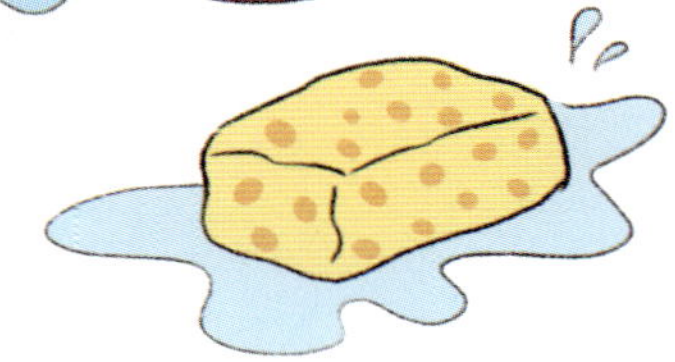

Mia is wondering where to start cleaning, while Mateo is already working. He rubs, rubs and rubs with all his strength, but the mud won't come off.
"It is so dirty!" said Mateo.
"Let me help you," replied Mia.
"No, it's too difficult for you," said Mateo.

Mia réfléchit par où commencer, tandis que Mateo se met au travail. Il frotte, frotte et frotte de toutes ses forces, mais la boue ne part pas.
– Que c'est sale ! dit Mateo.
– Laisse-moi t'aider, répond Mia.
– Non, c'est trop difficile pour toi, dit Mateo.

Suddenly, Mateo has an idea. He goes into the garage and finds the brush that Mommy uses for the grill.

Tout à coup, Mateo a une idée. Il va dans le garage chercher la brosse que Maman utilise pour le barbecue.

"What are you doing?" Mia asked her brother.
"Mommy says this brush removes all the dirt."
"AWESOME! Give it to me," said Mia.
Mia grabs the brush from her brother and they go back and forth.
"Let's take turns," said Mateo.

Mia demande à son frère :
– Qu'est-ce que tu fais ?
– Maman dit que cette brosse enlève toutes les saletés.
– GENIAL ! Donne-la moi, dit Mia.
Mia arrache la brosse des mains de son frère qui veut la lui reprendre.
– Chacun son tour, dit Mateo.

The two kids are trying with all their might to remove the mud. They scrub so hard that Mia's hat is covered with mud and Mateo's hair is dirty.

Les deux enfants mettent tous leurs efforts pour faire partir la boue. A tel point que le chapeau de Mia est couvert de boue et que Mateo en a plein les cheveux.

Suddenly, Mateo said: “Look Mia, the mud is gone and Daddy’s car has two colors now.”
“AWESOME! Red and gray looks so nice together. Daddy is going to be very happy.”
The twins are proud of their work.

Tout d’un coup, Mateo dit :
– Regarde Mia, la boue est partie et maintenant la voiture de Papa a deux couleurs.
– GENIAL ! C’est joli gris et rouge ensemble. Papa va être content.
Les jumeaux sont fiers de leur travail.

"DAAADDYYY! We are finished!"

"PAAAPAAA! On a fini!"

Daddy looks up and notices the scratches on his car. His hands fly to his head, with a confused look on his face. "What have you done?"

Papa arrive et constate les griffes sur sa voiture. Les mains sur la tête, le visage interrogatif.
– Qu'est-ce que vous avez fait?

"You said the car had to be clean. Mommy's brush removes all dirt, right Mia?" said Mateo, very proud of himself.

– Tu nous as dit que la voiture devait être propre. La brosse de Maman enlève toutes les taches, hein Mia ? dit Mateo très fier de lui.

“Yes. But it also removed the red paint!” cried Daddy. “Mommy’s metal brush has very strong bristles that should only be used on the grill. I wish you had checked with me before using it.”
“It’s AWESOME Daddy! We think your car looks better with two colors,” exclaimed Mia.

– Oui, peut-être, mais elle a aussi enlevé la peinture rouge ! répond Papa. La brosse métallique de Maman a des poils très durs et s’utilise uniquement sur le grill. J’aurais préféré que vous me demandiez l’autorisation.
– C’est GENIAL Papa ! Nous trouvons qu’avec deux couleurs ta voiture est plus jolie, s’exclame Mia.

"It's not exactly two colors. By using Mommy's hard brush, the red paint came off with the mud and the metal underneath is showing. Now, I have to take it to the body shop and have it repainted."
Daddy makes a phone call to Marc, the auto body technician.

– Ce n'est pas exactement deux couleurs. En utilisant la brosse dure de Maman, la peinture rouge est partie et c'est la carrosserie que l'on voit. Maintenant, je dois la porter au garage pour la faire repeindre.
Papa téléphone à Marc, le carrossier.

“I think we did something wrong,” whispered Mia.
“I know how to fix it, let’s get our paints!” said Mateo.

– Je crois qu’on a fait une bêtise, chuchote Mia.
– Je sais comment on peut faire; allons chercher notre peinture, dit Mateo.

“That is an AWESOME idea. Then Daddy will not have to go to the body shop.”
– Quelle idée GENIALE ! Papa ne devra plus aller au garage.

After his phone call, Daddy told the kids, "We are in luck! My friend Marc, the auto body technician, can repaint my car today."

"Daddy, it's not necessary anymore, we already painted the car for you," replied the twins.

Après son appel téléphonique, Papa dit aux enfants :

– Nous avons de la chance, mon ami Marc est carrossier et il peut repeindre ma voiture aujourd'hui.

– Papa, ce n'est plus nécessaire, on l'a déjà fait pour toi, répondent en cœur les jumeaux.

"What do you mean...? Oh my goodness!"
Mia and Mateo are surprised! They thought Daddy was going to reward them. Daddy sighed... "I know you are trying to help, but cars require a specific kind of paint. As I told you before, you should have asked permission first."
"Sorry Daddy," replied Mia and Mateo.

– Qu'est-ce que vous voulez dire... ? Ohlala !
Mia et Mateo sont étonnés ! Ils pensaient que Papa allait les féliciter.
Papa soupire...
– Je sais que vous avez voulu bien faire, mais la peinture pour voiture est spéciale. Comme je vous l'ai déjà dit, vous auriez dû me demander la permission.
– Pardon Papa ! répondent Mia et Mateo.

"Would you like to come with me to the body shop to see how cars are painted correctly?"
"Oh yes, please," exclaimed the twins. They all walked off to the car, and left for the shop.

– Voulez-vous venir avec moi au garage pour voir comment on peint correctement les voitures ?
– Oh oui, s'il-te-plaît, s'exclament les jumeaux. Ils marchent à grands pas vers la voiture pour aller chez le carrossier.

"Oh, there are the two little artists!" exclaimed Marc.
Mateo high fives Marc, the technician.

– Ah, voici les deux petits artistes ! s'exclame Marc.
Mateo tape la main de Marc, le carrossier.

Mia prefers a hand shake, like a big girl.
Marc leads them in and reports, "The red paint is ready, let's go."

Mia, comme une grande fille, préfère serrer la main.
Marc les laisse entrer et dit :
– La peinture rouge est prête, allons-y.

“Yikes! What has Marc put over his face?” asked Mateo.
Mia responds with confidence, “It’s to protect his face, right Daddy?”
“Yes, it’s always best to use proper equipment,” Daddy said, as Marc put on his safety glasses, mask, gloves and special suit.

– Beurk! Qu’est-ce que Marc a mis sur sa figure ? demande Mateo.
Mia, très sûre d’elle, répond:
– C’est pour protéger sa figure, hein Papa ?
– Exactement ! C’est toujours mieux de porter un équipement approprié, comme Marc qui a mis des lunettes spéciales, un masque, des gants et une combinaison pour se protéger.

While watching the auto body technician through the viewing window, Daddy explained the different steps.

Tout en regardant par une fenêtre ce que fait le carrossier, Papa explique les différentes étapes.

1. He uses sandpaper to remove the scratches.

1. Il utilise du papier de verre pour enlever les griffes.

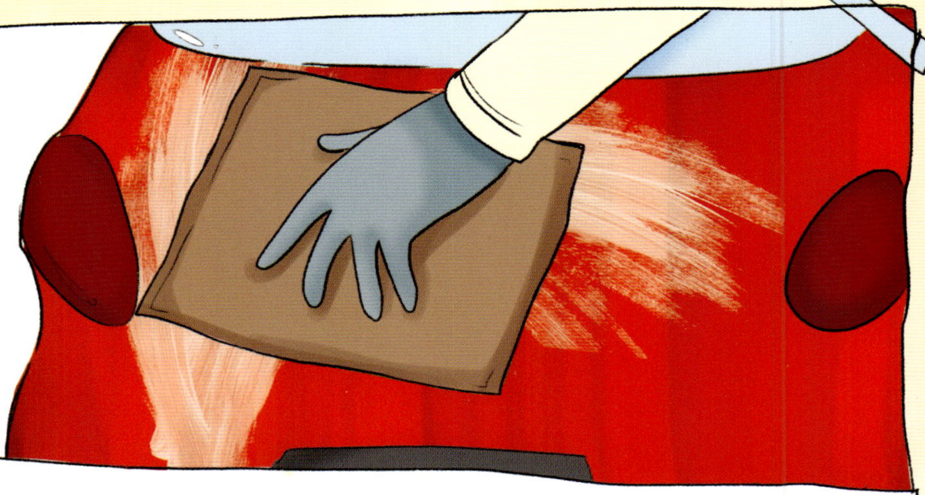

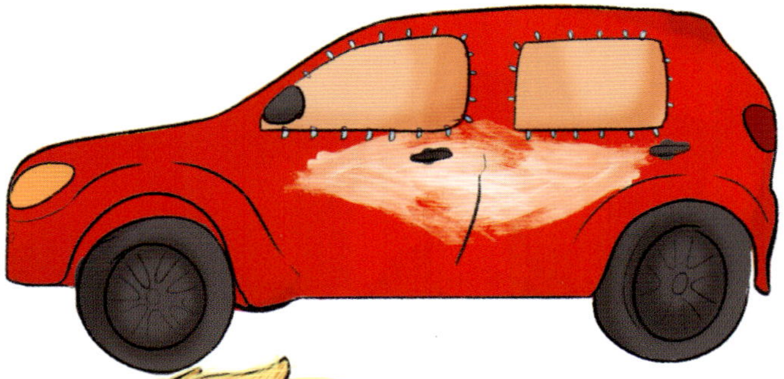

2. He places masking tape and paper to protect the rest of the car.

2. Il recouvre le reste de la voiture de papier brun et de papier collant pour la protéger.

3. He continues by spraying the primer.

3. Il continue par vaporiser la peinture de base.

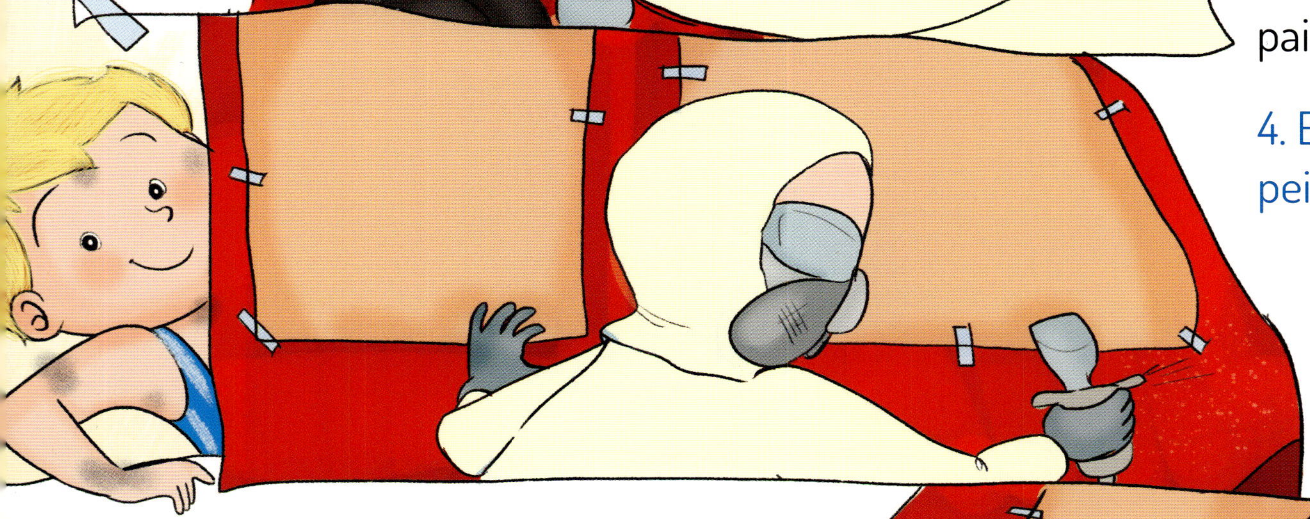

4. Then he applies the red paint.

4. Ensuite, il applique la peinture rouge.

5. And finally, he sprays clear paint, to make it shiny!

5. Et finalement, il vaporise la peinture transparente pour faire briller!

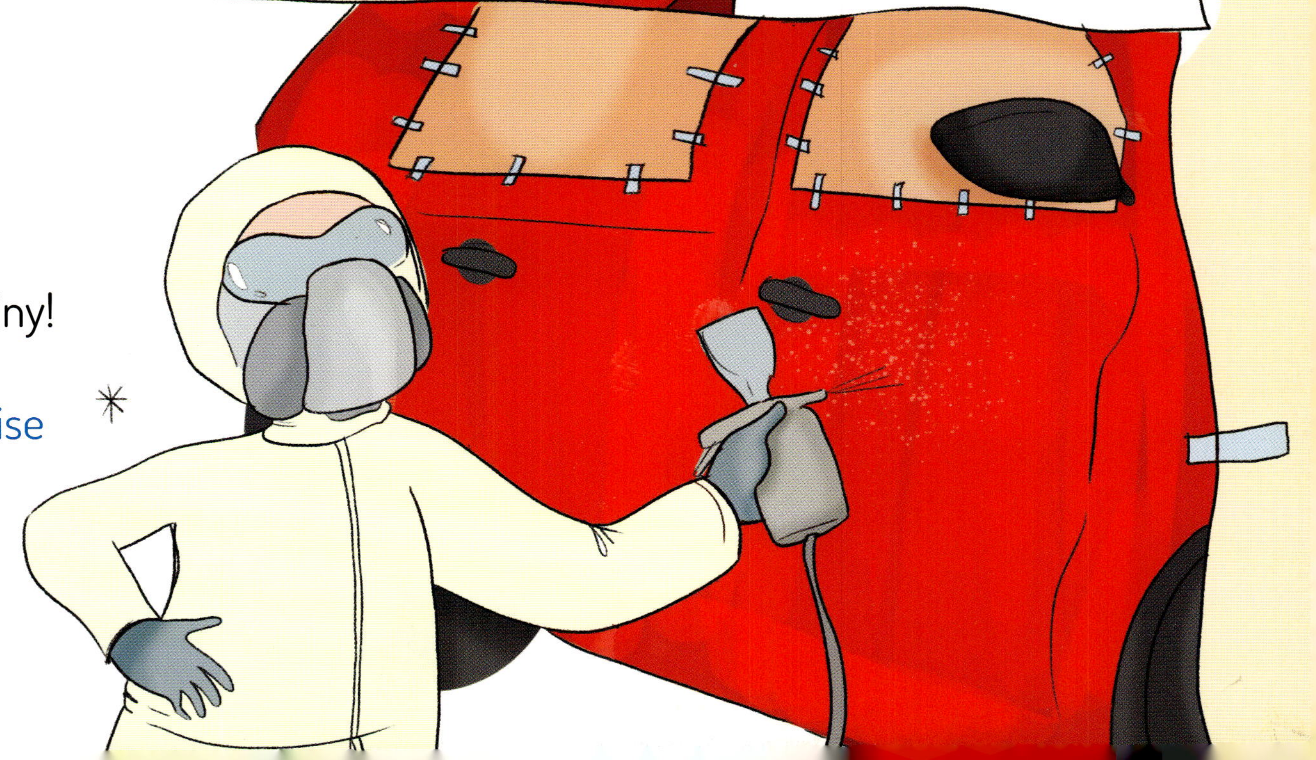

While the car is drying, Daddy and the twins went to get ice-cream.
"There you go, it is all done!" said Marc, as they reentered the shop.
Daddy is happy to see his car like new again.

Pendant que la voiture sèche, Papa et les jumeaux vont manger une crème à la glace.
– Voilà, c'est fait! dit Marc, lorsqu'ils arrivent au garage.
Papa est tout content de voir à nouveau sa voiture comme neuve.

"Come on kids! Let's share today's adventure with Mommy. She's not going to believe us."
"What a fun day, right Mia?" beamed Mateo.
"It was AWESOME! I love spending time with my brother and my Daddy."

– En route les enfants, allons raconter à Maman notre aventure d'aujourd'hui. Elle ne va pas nous croire !
– Quelle chouette journée, hein Mia ?
– C'était GENIAL! J'adore passer du temps avec mon frère et mon Papa.

Au revoir! A bientôt!
Goodbye! See you soon!

Woof
Woof

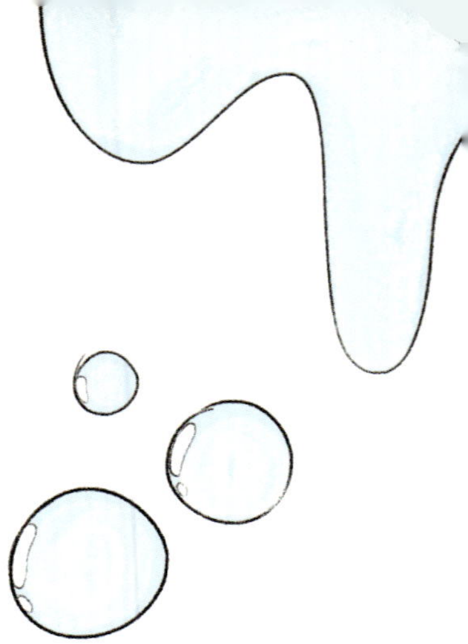

Auto body technician: le carrossier
Awesome: génial
Brother: le frère
Brush: la brosse
Bucket: le seau
Car: la voiture

Color: la couleur
Daddy: Papa
Dog: le chien
Face: le visage
Fun: amusant
Girl: la fille
Glasses: les lunettes

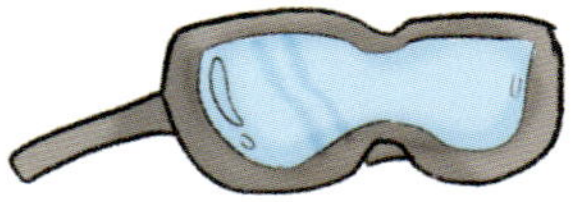

Grey: gris
Hair: les cheveux
Hand: la main
Happy: heureux
Hat: le chapeau
Head: la tête
House: la maison

Ice cream: la crème à la glace
Little: petit
Masking tape: le papier collant
Mommy: Maman
Mud: la boue
Paint: la peinture
Proud: fier
Red: rouge
Safe: sécurisant
Sandpaper: le papier de verre
Scratch: la griffe
Shine: brille
Sister: la sœur
Sponge: l'éponge
Strength: la force
Today: aujourd'hui
To remove: enlever
To scrub: frotter
To wash: laver
Twins: les jumeaux

Wouuff!
wouuff!